R

Advance Praise

'It's a rare thing to come across a debut collection as cohesive and accomplished as *Rotten Days in Late Summer*. Whether writing on love, class, illness, the working life, death or the complex and multi-faceted nature of human desire, Ralf Webb is never less than razor-sharp. With a storyteller's flair, he evokes a world of shifting terrains in which "anything could be an omen", and where refrains, motifs, stanza shapes and rhymes call to each other across the pages. In his extraordinary "Treetops" sequence, Webb navigates the labyrinths of mental illness and the ambiguous prize of health . . . It all feels gloriously, anarchically new'

Julia Copus, author of *This Rare Spirit:
A Life of Charlotte Mew*

'This is close-range language, magnifying without prejudice both the beautiful and the hard. Ralf Webb's poetry tells the truth of the push-pull of liberation and obligation . . . To work, to care, to mourn, but also to be a poet and queer and . . . dream of a commune in France – this is poetry in the grand tradition of annihilation by desire. It's what the young are always learning, and the old, if they are wise, never forget'

Anne Boyer, author of *The Undying*

'His poems take on grief and young manhood, and are largely set in England's West Country. "Accept this cheap and ironclad cynicism," Webb writes. "We're not famous. I am completely in love." The voice in this book is direct and heart-breaking. There's no pretension. It's all heart'

Alex Dimitrov, author of *Love and Other Poems*

ABOUT THE AUTHOR

Ralf Webb grew up in the West Country. He co-ran the *Swimmers* pamphlet and event series, and from 2017 to 2021 was managing editor of *The White Review*. Recently, he ran the Arts Council England-funded PoetryxClass reading group project. His writing has appeared widely, including in the *London Review of Books*, *Poetry Review*, *PAIN*, *Prototype*, *Hotel*, *Oxford Poetry* and *Fantastic Man*. This is his first collection.

RALF WEBB

Rotten Days in Late Summer

PENGUIN BOOKS

PENGUIN BOOKS

UK | USA | Canada | Ireland | Australia
India | New Zealand | South Africa

Penguin Books is part of the Penguin Random House group of companies
whose addresses can be found at global.penguinrandomhouse.com

First published 2021
001

Set in 10/13.75pt Warnock Pro
Typeset by Jouve (UK), Milton Keynes
Printed and bound in Great Britain by Clays Ltd, Elcograf S.p.A.

The authorized representative in the EEA is Penguin Random House Ireland,
Morrison Chambers, 32 Nassau Street, Dublin D02 YH68

A CIP catalogue record for this book is available from the British Library

ISBN: 978–0–141–99273–0

www.greenpenguin.co.uk

CONTENTS

A NOTE ON CONTENT

This book contains depictions of self-harm, suicidal thoughts and, in one case, homophobic violence. Readers who have struggled or are currently struggling with these issues may not wish to read this book alone, or without a trusted friend.

If you are having a difficult time, struggling to cope, or having thoughts about suicide, support is available 24 hours a day in the UK from the Samaritans (www.samaritans.org). Their free helpline can be called on 116 123.

If you have experienced biphobia, homophobia or transphobia in any setting, support is available from Galop (www.galop.org.uk) via their LGBT+ Hate Crime Helpline, Monday to Friday, 10:00am to 4:00pm, on 020 7704 2040.

Factotum, or *Suite for Nancy*

/

Hard work, it's hard work. These are the conditions.
The only thing that you can trust
is that it will be hard work.
The secret is not stopping:
past the industrial buildings, the mobile home parks
and motor shops, clear out beyond
the teetering Gulf garage,
she is three, four, five days on the road
carting boxes of medicinal creams
from care home to hospice,
repeating the pitch without thinking.
A bottle of two-in-one antifreeze sloshes
under the driver's seat.
Summer is a pink blur through the car windows.
Peculiar cloud formations, and dog-rose light.
It must be bad luck to spend so long
surrounded by the zoned ones,
in the houses of the half-living,
a pink smell crowding the corridors, flat and sweet.
Her defences might not mean a thing
(how many coins tossed in speculation
into stagnant wells, how many horseshoes
fixed, finally, over doors?),
but it's worth trying. The rabbit's foot,
tied to the rearview, sways.
There is a goodness here, somewhere,
there is sense in struggle:
the self-made are good, having struggled.
Under these conditions: back pain, cats eyes,

If You Are Feeling Tired, Please Pull Over.
She empties the ashtray through the window every dozen miles
and at red lights counts the cowry shells
bought from the fortune teller a week ago,
a year ago, in the Little Chef car park
off the A30, between the sea and nowhere.

/

A winch, a rusted chain slopped heavy
into an opened drain, purring.
Waterworks outside the care home.
The archeology needs purging, dredge,
to keep the surface firm and uniform.
Round the back, in the alley with the bad energy,
three neon bins say CHEMICAL WASTE:
UNSPECIFIED, and crows' heads rear
above the bus shelter, black and slick.
This is not insignificant. A new mobile mast
was erected recently, and cloaked
in fake foliage. Since it went up, the birds
have been acting off. And her headaches
are more frequent – the patients', too.
She begins to feel as if she can't move.
The shifts are scarce. The leaves have seemed
to yellow overnight, and there's a new,
underlying taste in the tap water. Something sour.
The secret: *thank you for my appraisal,*
I look forward to working toward my stated objectives.
Haul, and smile, and empty the old men's bedpans.
The kettle is on. It snarls with limescale.

/

This season she has been working door-to-door,
hawking home insulation. It's stopping
that's the hardest, especially in winter.
A valve closes, the machinery quits. And now
all the Christmas trees have been slung
on the curbs, heavy as children.
The people are more hostile.
She approaches each house like a spillage.
Good evening, my name is Nancy,
did you know there are many simple ways
to lower your heating bills? Cram the vacant cavities.
The doors open, just an inch,
and immediately slam shut. Sliding chains,
deadbolts. She understands.
Strangers are stranger in the cold.
Warm up in the car. Leave the engine idling.
She rakes a biro over the clipboard,
coaxing its ink to come unstuck
and tick off twenty homes: NO SALE.
Ice pellets fall from the heavy paunch
of January's newest storm.
They sink their black-and-white teeth
into the road, and hang on.
I am where I must be, for as long as I must be.
The rabbit's foot sways like a metronome.

White Ennox Lane

Take the road by the cluttered graveyard.
    Here, the dead stay dead.
    But the headstone moss is like stubble.

Take the track by the fenced-off woods.
    There is something that the trees are hiding.
    There are aerials in the trees.

Take the path by the abandoned quarry.
    The gates are guarded and wrapped in chains.
    The caves are more than caves: cities.

Take the lane by the trashed pillboxes.
    These enclosures were built to kill invaders.
    The horse-flies swarm the horse.

Aktiengesellschaft, Wiltshire

Green stuff has wormed its way up
through the mutilated tarmac
outside the main factory floor,
ultra-real in the neon warning lights.
New management have fortified protocol,
under the banner of 'efficiency'.
Lordly, alien, compulsory rules,
introduced by our friends
from Munich. Who visit occasionally.
Some of us walk to work. For others
home is an address spelled out
to a bank clerk. SEPA. BACS.
Easy enough to assemble. But when,
in free time, you feel impelled
to pick things apart, abstracts enter.
Like, Pete's looking at me funny, looks
kind of sinister, holding that spanner.
Is an accident ever an accident, or
a forced, subterranean lapse in judgement?
Automated warnings over the tannoy:
Do not attempt to clean the machine
from the inside. Do not attempt
to enter the machine. It's like they think
we're stupid. Who'd ever try that again?

Dawn Nurseries & Garden Co.

At the perennial nursery: Here Good
Soil Sold. Saturday,
midwinter, and buyers are scarce.
The few that pull up
are received passively,
like something administered.
A dog – it seems a stray –
sits on a stump, with its white eyes.

*

The widow who lived
in the dilapidated pebbledash bungalow
passed away two weeks ago.
The neighbours – thinking of this
as a generous grace period –
peer through the pane glass,
eyeing her antique rattan chair
and speculating about the will's executor.

*

A car parked beneath the overpass.
Cow shit, canisters and plastic bags.
The vehicle rocks; two fists
pop out of the sunroof and split open,
stiff fingers straining
for purchase. Nearby, scabs
of deserted machinery. A man,
all corduroy, crouched in the parsley.

Love Story: Rotten Days

I can see them, all my tools laid out
On the counter, hands hovering
Above them, trying to glean
The future of each. You understood
Their immediate functions, and moreover
Understood their functions in the final,
Abstract processes. The beginning
Of the night-shift: let loose
Our fantastic pissing contest.
A complete surrender to the overheads,
All of your blemishes lightened,
And grease in the corners of your mouth,
Your stalled moustache. The moths
And May bugs, ending themselves.

Processes: provide us with meaningful
Ligatures, that we might tie
Our gnawed hands together, and hoover
The millions of metal filings in unison.
Swarf stuck in our skin like ticks.
And, boy, would we brag about it.
I categorised the cleaning liquids
According to colour. The green
Was my favourite, more pine than pine:
I was a pioneer, cleaning the toilets,
As if scrubbing away the shit
Of tired men would impress you.
And when the heat got too much:
Please, let's stop, I'm running on empty –

You would never feel so powerful as then,
Rolling one, another, slurping water.
I didn't understand what it meant,
That need I had to have you lift
The awful weight of the archaic wrench,
And beat raw my pampered limbs
Beside the big machine, with its weeping oils.
I still don't know if it was real,
Your truant intelligence, which I thought
A physical intelligence, a kind
Of architecture. But I wanted it,
Whatever it was, to rub off on me
Like the transference of powder
From moth's wings to thumb and finger.

Secondary Education

Somebody's spray painted WARNING: ASBESTOS
on the side of the slumped storage shed,
by the bike stands. She doesn't know if it's a prank,
or what. Structural integrity
as an open question . . . ? Sort of funny.

Emily's thinking about Business Studies.
Like, how quickly can she turn a profit
on this ounce of weed? The target demographic:
lunchtime boys, in black jackets,
with their crumpled tenners and moon-eyes.

White Widow. Resin-heavy. What branding.
A friend in need's a friend indeed.
It's about selling a story: reliably clad in leather,
so that the misfits trust her,
while everyone else leaves well enough alone.

After break, slouching in German class:
Gestern nach der schule, habe ich gearbeitet . . .
at the chicken factory. Herr Barker
is losing the faith. Does Emily have no ideas.
How do you say 'hair net' in Deutsch?

In the middle of the vocabulary test, Steve shoves
his hands down his trousers, the prick,
and threatens to 'show it her'.
There are thirty students in the room.
Every one of them, and Barker, keep shtum.

Education, education, *und so weiter*.
People are always telling her, *cheer up love, it might
never happen*. Emily's never known what 'it' is.
At the final bell, she takes great care
pushing pins into Steve's back tyre.

Crash

Copper stench, low-frequency fly-drone:
a body in the hedgerow. It drapes
out of the windscreen like a rubber prop.
Drawn by the noise, a man appears
wearing nicotined overalls.
And others come.
Inching closer, these men take photographs.
At first they thought the driver
was the local doctor. The bloodied back
of his head: a similar combover.
Someone said they'd seen him slip a bottle
from his glove box, once.
But Dr Miller didn't drive such a car.
Wouldn't wear a suit like that –
with all them frills.
Just a stranger, then. Not from round here.
Sirens doppler sluggish down the lanes.
Cause: the radiant heart
that ran his body stuttered, suddenly.
He lost control, and the car overturned.
Things, slowly, are put back to normal:
the hedgerow, hiding a plot of untilled land,
between the derelict inn and valve factory.
A waste, really. Everyone says its soil's good for growing.

The Country Manor Hotel

Spry, pink, the Proprietor stalks
through rows of regimented trees
which stand stately and erect,
as though poised to march.
These are new woods planted
with hunting in mind.
He has twinned the cults of Diana
and Property Law, and patrols,
obsessively, the length of the boundary.

He knows, most Sundays, local kids
like to toy with a fly-tipped scrap heap
in a ditch at the edge of his estate,
fighting to be throned King or Queen
of the defunct Hotpoint washing machine.
Their weapons: clods and stones.
Rations: windfalls, pinched off his orchard.
He kneels, half-hidden, to aim and shoot
at the thought-clouds above their heads . . .

It has become as bothersome
as scattering birds. Still, he gets a shiver
of pleasure, a little ripple in the groin,
at seeing their brittle limbs break for cover.
Back in the kitchen of the Manor Hotel,
salt is flung at the raw, plummy flesh
of a dismantled muntjac. It is right,
he thinks, for a Proprietor to feature
meat from his own land on the menu.

He spent millions refurbishing the Manor.
Restoring the period features,
stuffing mod-cons in the innards.
It profited him. City couples
fill the rooms throughout the year.
They want *authentic* country.
First class everything. Like anyone with sense,
he understands you won't catch prey
by waiting for it to fall at your feet.

You Can't Trust Violence

Daniel is washing lilac from the windscreen –
Daniel meaning *God Is My Judge.*
Church is a chore, like taking the bins out.
If Daniel complains, Dad says:
I don't work twelve-hour days to keep the roof
above the head of a fucking poof.
Yes Sir, Phil Sir. Keys in the ignition.
Maybe there are no right paths,
only wrong destinations.
A cold summer at seventeen:
teeth in the gristle. Foil trays
glazed with monosodium glutamate.
At The Royal Oak with the others,
someone hijacks the aux, and flicks on the strobe.
This is an approximation of freedom,
the flashes of metal and gums. Daniel,
dancing half-ironically to lo-fi house.
Three pints, two blunts, bad apples.
Whose round is it. Who's not out of pocket.
'Are You Struggling With Debt?' – the Moneylender.
'If you're owed a fiver you've lost a fiver' – Sir Phil.
Later, laughter in the car park, the sound
of a tyre leaking its air.
That kid with the long hair's over there,
by the wisteria. What's-his-face, from the year below,
with the beads around his neck.

In Daniel's mind's eye, a road opens up, running
from the car park, across the flood plain,
like a line bisecting the giant hand of God.
Daniel's head is about to pop.

The excuse being, anything different.
What would it feel like:
a metal pipe, slapped into an open palm,
then elevated, then struck down,
into the mouth of that queer.
Dear Dad, Sir, it would be so pretty,
the wincing crunching jewellery.
God's hand closes and makes a fist.
The path folds in on itself. Keys, ignition.
Daniel thinks that justice is a feeling,
potted and tended by fathers,
and passed down along a line. It flowers
when it's supposed to flower.
Justice isn't a load of words in a book.
Five minutes on the lane, and everything . . .
starts . . . spinning . . . He pulls in at the petrol station.
Suddenly, Daniel sicks chicken chow mein
down his front, and down again,
all over his shoes. Hyper–hiccup–ventilation.
The brand new Nikes that Phil bought him.
Who'll claim remittance.
Using both hands, and implements.

The Chicken Witnesses

After school one Friday, at Jack's parents' house,
with someone like Leonard Cohen or Rodriguez on the record
    player,
we heated up hash and wondered out loud
about what it means to 'pay your dues',
which animals our souls resembled most,
and the viability of Alice's thought
from the house party, last week, to move the best of us to France
and establish a commune, building homes from mud and tyres.
Wherever in France, she'd specified, then whitied.
To live off the land. The idea entranced us.

Jack was in the very back of the garden, checking
on the beehives his dad had installed –
an anoraky venture, and new, that allowed him to play
as the town's laconic, worldly gentleman,
able, through studied kinship with the hive,
to glean and sell edible sunlight.
Jack yelled, *One of the chickens is dead.*
We stepped outside and saw him lift it by its feet,
wafting bees off with his one free hand
in faithful imitation of a beekeeper's son.

Not a mark on her, he said, *not a single mark.*
We thought this ruled out attack by fox,
but according to Alice, merely *seeing* such a predator
can make a chicken's tiny heart explode.
Even so, we began to imagine an invisible syndrome,
pernicious, parasitic, which had stalked through the garden
in search of a host, and might, like a spirit,
seep from the bird-body and, without warning,

into any one of us. We put out the spliff we were smoking:
it felt discordant, somehow, to get high in front of the chicken.

The bird had gone hard. Jack taught us new words:
rigor mortis. It was getting dark,
the summer kind of dark that feels incidental and safe.
So we wrapped the chicken in a towel and took it to The Pigs.
There was a temptation to make jokes, like,
and a pint for our feathered friend, but a seriousness had set in.
Not maudlin, exactly, but a feeling that our lives
were on a particular track, and the direction needed righting.
Back then, our ideas had no ceilings. But only because
we hadn't yet built a room for them to break free from.

We talked loudly, obnoxiously, over the drinks,
to muffle our nerves, and to hide the fear
that we had done wrong by this animal's soul,
and our actions might count in an afterlife.
Then went back to pick up a bucket and spade.
In the kitchen, Jack's mum kept bowls of spoiled fruit,
whited with mould. It used to seem that she couldn't face
the inevitability of waste – but that night
her collection was a menagerie of decay,
a celebration of matter's transience.

We dug a hole in the common, and lowered in the bird.
Its feet sprouted from the earth, like a child's solution
to the paradox of *what came first?*
Then a voice barked from the footpath:
What do you think you're doing? Some suit from the new-builds,
walking his dog. *Fuck off, we're burying a chicken.*

Our voices seemed to stretch all the way across the valley.
Not so much an echo, as an expression too enormous
and unstable to be held within the usual parameters.
We dropped to all fours and started in with the dirt.

Love Story: Boys at the Age of Twenty

That month you grew out your beard
And I self-medicated, homesick,
With a thorough love of you,
Which was neither brotherly nor obtuse
But like a stone jar, into which I poured
Everything molten and rash.
Your sides hurt from all the splitting,
Crow's feet formed by the relentless
Lack of cloud cover. You bragged
That your tortoiseshell frames
Were hand-me-downs from your grandmother,
And they were. But not for the seeing.
Something more talismanic, and shallow.
(We were practised in recycling our dead.)

I was lean, wore only vests, and counted
Day after day the bug bites which began
At our knuckles, and spread downwards,
Across our bellies. No matter
How far I went (and it was the easiest
Thing in the world, to be crass)
I wasn't the man you wanted me to be.
The bites kept appearing. Protests
Against our intrusive bodies, the way
We would fit them into any situation,
Without thinking, without needing to think.
The comfort zone started crumbling.
Thumb in my mouth, at the foot of your bed,
I whispered: *I'm writing you a love song.*

We left, to stop our mouths with the sea.
And started talking only in quotes,
References to our favourite episodes:
You'll have to speak up, I'm wearing a towel!
My appetite went. No to the pizzerias.
No, no spaghetti either. Instead,
I preened orange peels, looking
For new thoughts. I was wet linen
Strung on sticks; you grew bigger.
Like a galleon you risked the water,
And won, diving all the way down
To the living floor, hunting for treasure.
I unravelled on ashy rocks, picking scabs
And licking baked salt from my biceps.

Contaminates and their Sources

We have found ourselves together
in the car, at night.
With a shift each in the morning.
Followed by a lesson in fire safety.
With a shift, both.
And then my taking leave of here.
I can see you have forgotten how to steer.
We are laughing, though it hurts to,
and the idea of it hurts.
The car halts by the polluted swamp.
Hazard lights, and the radio playing.
It was embarrassing, watching you try to steer.
We are throwing car doors wide open
and proceeding with the routine
crumbling of leaves.
I am not deserving of this flaming branch,
and you are less deserving.
The beautiful swamp is green and disturbing.
We are pitching crushed cans
into its burnt surface.
Which doesn't want to reflect us.
I'm announcing that it feels pretty weird
to be insignificant, and have
things wrong inside the head.
And unknowns, elsewhere (tapping
at my chest). To have wrongs
and unknowns, and be of little consequence.

Dogging Is a Love Poem

The slow river is gold in the dusk.
Cattle graze, and rest.
A tinny car stereo echoes out,
somewhere deep in the valley.
You know you shook me, baby.
Bonfires spark across the hills.
Pints are pulled in free houses.
The regulars are as pink as apples.
The stereo shakes itself out.
You shook me so hard, baby.
Night slopes in, like drunkenness.
Headlights and torchlights foam
over the hidden meadow, and roe.
Baby, baby, please come home.
Night leaks like sap, like mucus.

Love Story: Lies

It wasn't fair, to have attempted to bury
Everything – every wager I'd ever
Made, each part of my body
Ever bartered – through the act
Of settling my chin, pitiable and heavy-hearted,
Into your armpit. I believed
There was something respectable –
And god, I wanted to feel good
Like that – in deliberate self-censorship.
Eating ice cream, comparing
Each other's handwriting: here,
Take all my edits, keep what's useful,
But forget the rest. Do it quickly.
I don't want us to have time to think.

Playing house was fun, because we could
Dissect the rules of the game
With eloquence, and knew how to invert them,
But never really did. Which in itself
Felt sort of subversive. And how
Can anyone be sad, flossing
At two a.m., with the bare foot
Of someone they're supposed to love
At rest upon their own bare foot? Spitting blood:
The right way to do it. A few screams
From the neighbours, sure, and the flatmate
Has locked himself in his room
For the better part of a week, totally dosed . . .
But, wow, we're really here, aren't we.

It wasn't a pose, exactly, but an aspiration,
As rigid and obsessively scrutinized
As my bone structure. I tried
To build you up, and latch on, so that
I would be built up in turn. Tending
To noodles, rating moisturizers, waiting
For winter to be over: I was rudderless,
Convincing you of things I couldn't believe
Myself: 'Wanted to say, just wanted
You to know, I'll lose this baby-fat eventually.
Slow down, I promise, we've time.'
It wasn't obvious when it began to disappear.
Half-asleep one night, I started,
Realizing it was no longer there.

Diagnostics

How are we feeling today, the nurses will say to him, in hospital.

At some point we will begin to adopt the use of the first person plural. We will ask ourselves: *How are we?*

Throughout his adult life, a life, in large part, of work, uncertainty and struggle, he is paranoid about getting sick. Both his father and paternal grandfather passed away from cancer in their fifties. He is heard, more than once, to say *I won't live past fifty-five.*

It seems like fate.

We, his family, orbit him, the collie at our side.

The hire: teaching at the new school.
For the foreseeable. No more *I don't know
what comes next*, no briefcase dropped,
pettily, to stone. Still stretched, but less.
The wires on the rotary washer are slacker: bless
this skinny effigy, opposed to downpours.
Racing home from his first week, he takes a bad fall
on black ice, and snaps his bike in two.
Thirty miles per hour. *Thwack.* The oozing roses.
Recovery is quick enough, but still,
the fall proves to have been like a tablecloth
whipped away, leaving all glassware
intact, and a teetering that never stopped.
He develops a twitch in the eyes, and quits
the rituals he no longer understands:
bins his cigarettes, and frees up time
to really get to grips with drinking.
There is no correct place to begin, or end:
he buys a pair of glasses with enormous frames,
and just gets back to work. Has had no sick days,
for two decades. A person out of time,
now slipping, unnoticed, into change:
there is no correct place to end, or begin.

We believe that sustained individual happiness is a flouting of the natural order of things, of the teeth-gritting, the monotony, the ordinary hunger and long hours. Deviation will be met with punishment.

He is fifty-four. More than ever, he is happy. Stability and contentment are in his grasp.

Revisiting the old photographs, later, we will notice with surprise how skinny he had already looked. How long had the sickness been in him? How did we not see? The sweat pours out.

For now, all of us are a little bit worried. We can't yet metabolize more than that.

Aren't you tired of walking around in circles?
After years of routine, he has ditched
his hoop and stick, and steps forward
onto unclouded ground. Just as
he finds his footing, there is a seizure:
terrible contracts are found in the fluid.
A suitcase is packed with remarkable speed.
Shoddily, but, still. Zip. Vroom. In-patient.
The tread on the car tyres is wearing thin.
It is inconceivable, until it happens, and then
seems as inevitable as losing a chess game:
the fissured heads of superior pieces,
having made sacrifice of weaker blood,
ratchet themselves into tighter positions
and advance, lunatics, into fatal gridlock.

In the early stages of the chemotherapy there are gaps: moments when the carousel stops spinning, and he can get off to stretch his legs in the long grass.

The doctors introduce us to new words, or already-known words to which they have attached better definitions: Blast Cells. Cell Count. Remission. Consolidation.

We are surprised that his treatment and medication forbid him to eat grapefruit, but allow him to drink alcohol.

In these pauses, the family can gather in stillness. We have stopped running around. Here, we are comforted by the temporary possibility of a gentler outcome. Ugly, normal fear does not exist. In a way, it is the most peaceful any of us has ever felt.

Would he call it contentment, these
lighted pillars, and outlines
of happy heads in beer glasses
at the village inn by the house,
the shadows of those heads
ferociously dark and animated
against delaminated stucco,
immune in their opaqueness
to the night glares? Lovely,
lovely anaesthetics . . . This evening,
all of us are safely landed.
The bloods are still in transit.
But simply being here
is cause for celebration.
Take a minute. Untie your tongue.
The peeled sun, setting, oozes
in bitter dregs. It cracks itself
over everyone's screens.
Pockets rattle with pocket change.

After some weeks he is moved to a different, specialist wing, in a Victorian building concealed behind the modern ward.

This older wing is confusing. We take a wrong turn. We walk along the wrong corridor. The air smells like urine, antiseptic and copper. Through the gaps in half-pulled cubicle curtains, we see the balding, flaking heads of two dozen people, each connected to tubing. But when we calm down, our thoughts grow. None of the people who are sick, none of their family and friends, *have* to be here. That we are marks a common faith in the basic value of existence.

We are all of us going to pieces. He tugs at the annoying cannula.

It could be anywhere. A brightly lit room,
with plain furniture, and machines
attached to the walls, completing revolutions.
Inside, frustrated, he knocks himself against
hard surfaces, or else stands perfectly still
and loose-jawed, palms extended: hoping
that something might come to bristle
through the cold air's grain, and ignite it,
and wake him thoroughly up,
who cannot remember his own PIN.
Twenty-five years of teaching:
suddenly, nobody can read his handwriting.
Days hover around his eyes, scavengers,
and pour into them. Then back out again.
Marrow is drained, replaced, like engine oil.

The treatment doesn't work. This information arrives to us like rumour, passed along a chain. One of us is mowing the grass, having known for several days, while another sits in the attic, completely unaware, idly sketching flowers in pencil on the wooden beams.

Nobody wants to be the one to bring the catastrophe into consensus, and thereby into reality. It is two weeks before the truth spreads from the doctor, through his sister, then his children's mother, to his children. (The collie, we suspect, has known for some time.)

Then we are shy, wishy-washy, in front of the weight of 'terminal'. We are given leaflets that speak of *Managing Pain*, *Withdrawing Treatment* and *Coping Financially*. It rushes forward, at us. The weeks, which were already short, become shorter.

The midnight handbrake in the summer driveway,
wrenched, bearing bad news;
flying insects amass and whirl
in front of the headlights, like inverted snow,
and someone who he loves dearly
says that they have their drinking under control.
At last the pink moon is unregulated
and the voices in the other room are fearful;
there is sadness in a process started
that cannot be reversed, or even paused.
But the collie, anyway, has shot free over the brick wall
and bounds like a sea creature through the dark crop.

He wants his last words, his imaginary final language, to contain and communicate everything. Every page of his life, every page of the shadow lives he has lived in dreams. Time slows down. The sounds he makes are like butterflies trapped in a room at the height of summer, flying again and again into a shut window. The room is stuffy, close. The glass is clear. They hammer and vibrate like this, against the solid glass. They are trying to reach the outside; they want to subsume and be subsumed by everything that is in the outside, and to share this experience with others. Love is the driver of this need.

(If only he had health enough to smash the glass, or to burn down the room, or to call the outside inside.)

We have been waiting for this day, and have become so accustomed to the waiting that when it arrives we can no longer be roused in time.

Don't worry. *I'm not turning religious,*
or anything. Hallucinations
of white dogs snuffling for truffles
under the care-at-home bed. Pink, pink, pink
shapes, shapes like coins, dangling
in the window. The fruit tree in the garden,
dropping plums, because it is
September. There are notes
on the mantel, in envelopes,
for the children. A spider wrote them.
The children are not here. It is raining where
they are, scrambling to the train station,
with their mother, *come now,*
it's now, come. It. I. Snow. It is September.
The pronoun vaults, vibrates, and turns
into vapour. After that,
the floor is not there any more.

Together, in the aftermath, we develop the Radiation Theory: the longer one exposes themself to memories of his sickness, the greater the risk of contracting one's own. We do not talk about it. We do not think about it. We will not risk exposure.

So the memories of him are cordoned off. They become an exclusion zone. Because they are not tended to, new ecologies develop there, flourishing and mutating at accelerated speeds.

Something is forming inside each of us, something is taking hold. We had touched him, and it did nothing to help. Maybe it made things worse. Maybe we put the plastic gloves on wrong, or didn't affix the face masks properly; maybe we carried in some germ which finally destroyed his tattered immune system.

The consensus begins to erode. Each person judges the other for the direction the undertow pulls them in. At night, alone in our rooms, we listen in case his voice speaks out. Some hoard clothes and discount vouchers, and let the gutters clog.

Others begin to beatify him: he becomes the Saint with the Sheepdog. Stories of his youth are sought out and exaggerated, if not entirely fabricated. He is the Angry Young Man in drainpipes, in leather. Some of us want to be acolytes, and so emulate these stories: we stop watching our speed, and drink until we are incapacitated.

Rotating around a fixed axis, every
cord yoked to another,
and pulled incredibly tight.
His son has gifted himself
the cheapest, best bottles.
Unscrewing them is a peaceable deadening
of the harsh inner sounds:
dewclaws on linoleum floors, shrapnel
peeling the scratch-cards.
Then, the days are cut loose,
like reddened ribbon, and thresh
in unrehearsed weather.
At twenty-one, he is photographed
huffing from a paper bag at night,
at a funfair, somewhere far away
from the house, and the family.
His neck muscles are strained
in toothy gurning, a structure artlessly
detaching itself from his self.

Then the collie becomes sick. Some of us think that this is proof of the Radiation Theory, that the dog's sickness is a double-happening, an echo: the dog dwelled for too long in thoughts of him.

Others among us don't believe that the sickness could be so malicious as to transmit itself to an innocent animal. And in this thinking, we realize that we have, all along, attributed conscious intent to the sickness. We have instilled it with malevolence, with evil sentience. In naming this thought, we realize how absurd it is.

The collie has been eating grass all morning.
The growth atop his head has forced
his right eye partly out of its socket.
Imagine the pressure. Poor boy.
That night, his dark fur glinting
like onyx in the moonlight, he digs a hole
beside the compost. In the kitchen,
fat is burning a second skin
onto the frying pan; someone calls him in.
And then he lunges. His canines and claws
have always looked like a wolf's.
It's the pain made him do it.
He's no longer himself. *Poor boy.*
The next day we have him killed.
Then sit fuzzy-headed outside Costa,
with foam and chocolate. And hairs
from his coat, blue merle, caught
on our sleeves. We pluck every strand,
and fold them inside napkins,
which we stow in our breast pockets.

We scatter the collie's ashes where we had scattered his.

There is no 'we' any more. Whatever had taken hold became a solid mass, expanding outward, pushing us further from one another.

As clichéd as it is, the days go by. The leaves quake, and the mass stops expanding. It can be looked upon lucidly. *How much time has passed? How far have you come? How long ago did you paint the room white – a year? Ten?* The paint is going yellow in the corners. It is time for something new.

I see signs: when the light is good, I scan the landscape for balusters and aqueducts, for the columns that support the order of things, and tread accordingly. It is like learning a new language, a learning that will go on for ever.

But we will gather together again. When we do, we will, privately, have returned to the memories of him. The brighter patterns within those memories will be newly legible, and newly sustaining.

Time, almost, to leave the house,
that fickle husband. Where
does all this water come from?
The last man broke a promise
about the sealants. Cf. floating leaves,
confetti. Off with the husband.
The lane that curves to the lamppost:
nobody is there, crooked against dry stone
sneaking a last cigarette,
before coming in from the long night.
The hiccoughing moths. How routine,
this warped way of looking.
The kitchen sink, drip, is big enough
to bathe a puppy. Where does all
the residue go? In the piping,
in the back of the head, something dislodged.
And what came pouring out, holy –

Love Story: The Back Pages

Your mouth is different from how I
Remember it. Shall I write this?
There is a new redness to your mouth.
Language slopes from its side, barely audible,
Self-satisfied: as though one morning,
Shirtless, you awoke to a room
That was not home, and the sound of rain,
And here discovered the rendition
Of yourself that pleased you most,
And have remained pleased since, and so
Speak inconsiderately, as somebody pleased.
You are still thinner than me.
(Shall I write this redness.)
In Caterpillar boots. Haloed with Bose.

It's been several years at least.
And now, we're stuck in this carriage together
By accident, I guess, and for the duration.
And we compare commuting habits,
Like, what type of playlists.
Which seems dumb. And when the train
Stops by the hospital you ask, Is this You?
It isn't me. And when the train stops by
The romantic Victorian terrace I ask,
Is this You? Obviously not.
We are both en route to the total core –
Can you believe it? Pretty mature –
Where you'll turn right, and I'll turn left,
Cementing the tradition.

It's funny – bad funny – growing old,
But still being young:
One day ten years ago I was laying my head
On your chest, in the stupid meadow,
Actually chewing grass and thinking about
The ruby slopes, your parents' record collection,
The lavender smell of your sweatshirt,
And now here you are: a muffled snowman
In an outsize mac acting like you hardly know me.
Like, altercation, what altercation.
Well I will write: I am so tired,
And so green, and have violent
Dreams occasionally. Tell me what happens.
Please. Before we reach the ticket barrier.

Fox the Talking Head

after 'Fox and His Friends', dir. Fassbinder

My compatriots have all quit. Left for Paris,
or prison. The cashbox got confiscated.
If the word is repeated often enough,
you don't even know what it means any more:
Cash-in. Cash-up. Cash-rich. Cash-strapped.
All I had left, I kept inside my sock.

And then I got lucky, which I deserved,
as much as anyone deserves anything.
I've waited my whole life to get lucky.
Still, I stayed unwashed – why wash? – until
the new men began to flatter me. It's tough
to distrust flattery, when it seems sincere.

I fell in love. This kind of love was an economy.
I didn't realize that 'ours' meant 'his',
so I bought us everything that he wanted.
That stuff didn't matter. Only his happiness.
They don't tell you that a man doesn't have
a tidy head just because he has a tidy closet.

Learn, learn, learn, he said. And I tried my best.
I climbed the carpeted stairs, wearing
the correct slippers, and ashed in the right places.
It's like my kindness was a fly, trapped inside a jar,
and his hand was wrapped around the jar.
Cream suits and antiques . . . I made such an effort.

God, chief, so many people are closed-hearted.
What is a heart but a muscle, and blood
a type of currency? He siphoned my blood,
and ate up my muscle, with a turtle soup.
I watched him do it. Signed my name on the line.
Everyone's to be had. What a pity.

Cultural Studies

It will happen to many of our friends:
they will begin to pace
in perfect circles, and will not stop,
chewing their lips or the insides
of their mouths. Some will become
very tired, others more or less unconscious,
all will have their heads slumped
and drag their feet as though leashed
to a stone pillar in the centre
of the circle, as though pacing in order
to rotate that pillar, and cause
colossal but meaningless shifts
in the plates of the earth,
where we all live.
Looking on, we will want
to sever the circle, and this need will settle
down to a dull and persistent ache,
getting harder and cooler each day.
But it will take something thoroughly
inventive, something terrifying and selfless
to sever it. Like a flaming horse
crashing through sheet rain, like a UFO
floating above the village green.
Something miraculous like that.
Which would change the meaning of things.
If such a thing arrived, perhaps
we would reject it, being wary of change.

Apparent Retrograde Motion

Your new wingtips are having difficulties.
It would be polite not to demand a knife,
but the constant slippage is killing you, so.
Wasps. Papers stuck together. Humidity
and spilt liquor. To the waiter: *A light? A knife?*
Your double-barrelled acquaintances arrive,
whom I must absolutely, apparently,
one hundred percent meet. They're on *good form*:
flawless, Class A form. And everybody knows
creatives love to drink. So begins the oratory . . .
Sad boy, blonde locks, posing with Negroni:
I'm sick of burning the midnight oil, in these,
the final days. Grouped around a circular bench,
with cups, they try to parse the planetary signs,
on phones. Looking for a place to lay the blame.
There isn't one. There are too many.
Most of them have money, actually.
But some of them don't. It's getting harder
to tell the difference. The uncertainty creates
a tightness in the chest. Let's change the topic
to Pain Relief, please! *Our dear X died,*
aged twenty-three, from an overdose . . .
You nosedive into powdery gossip
about the infamously perverted flâneurs,
the New York critic and book editors
that your halting career orbits.
Cue the false outrage: cue the dropped jaws.
I find the men's room and make myself sick.

Love Story: Dettol Protects

I time my outbursts against the clock
Above the bar at the pub, where you work.
For ten whole minutes I will lock
My better qualities inside a basement,
And belt them. And go out of my way
To make you miserable. For example:
Creeping in at last orders, all proud,
All injured. Teeth from ear to ear,
With something hidden under my sleeve . . .
Self-flagellation in private, made,
Tactfully, public! I am experimenting
In hurt, learning how to be cruel
To myself, and others. Better still,
Learning how to be original.

Sit on the edge of the tub, and slowly
Undress me, then gently dress
The holes I've scissored straight into
The costume I designed for you
(Using your notes: New Romantic, idiot)
And the definite holes that I have punched
Into myself. But I'll only let it
Go on for a minute, before I admit,
This is really pathetic. Don't do it.
Don't dab the compress in Dettol,
Don't ask, nicely, if it stings. Jab, instead.
Horrible, this unlit reservoir of
The heart, which desperately wants you
To despise me, but refuses to let you go.

It's not that simple. We both of us relished
The taste of the other's blood.
Isn't the best way to debase someone
To imitate their worst traits back at them?
A combination of mimesis and pantomime.
While I was buttering my knives
You were starving yourself, in secret.
Really pulling your hair out. Every night,
By the light of the silvery moon,
Our delirious sort of fucking:
A cat toying with a mouse, or a mouse
Playing dead for the cat, while the house
Burns down all around them. It's alright.
The doorknob still works. Say leave, and I'll leave.

Treetops

Referring to the notes I took. The tapes.
Looking for all my pieces – *gotta find*
those missing pieces! – before the floor
gives out. I'm upstairs, a window is open.
Men without faces speak in tongues
in the street. Can that be right?
Take off those masks, I think,
I'm trying to work! Shucks to these distractions.

Am committed, cross my heart and hope to die,
to the task. Have spent days, weeks,
searching the light on my wall –
images of people I once knew, who were
once new, perfectly composed
and in fabricated contexts (God,
how many rides in aeroplanes! Sunsets,
Perpetua) – looking for the right answers.

It is difficult, now, to pronounce their names.
Patterns emerge, like seeing forms
in clouds, hearing broadcasts
in crashing waves . . . In this photo,
somebody's head has been sliced clean off
by a fingertip obscuring the lens.
Ah! Get it off! Rinse this light
down the drain, rinse away all this information.

My dear beheaded, where did all our roads
diverge? The blue roads and golden rod,
the white branches I hacked at
without mercy. The logic of trees . . .
unfurling fractals. It's easy to trace

our present backwards, replaying the memories
frame by frame. There's even [breathe]
some comfort in it, despite the resulting sightlessness.

But the opposite is impossible:
to have guessed exactly *how* we would go
through the necessary filters:
cold coffee, Big Pharma, burst capillaries.
O, times are hard. I owe you all a message
from my early twenties: *Sorry for the delay,*
got your email, then spent the next five years
staring out the window, hope all's well –

but it seems there is no ribbon left.
Jammed keys. The knowledge that
nearly a decade – a decade – has gone
[a tape measure snapping home]
since we packed the suits,
the sunflowers, queasily away.
And still these ailments are not a phase.
Still, most days, I am shook, shaking,

detaching limbs from other limbs,
to reattach them in a new way.
Confounded plastics, cheap machinery.
The pieces never fit together properly.
Click. Clack. Whoops – there goes
the little wad of absolute pain,
it's fallen from its cage again, and is rolling
like a cue ball across the floorboards,

settling under the dresser, with the cobwebs.
It'll stay there, I suppose, for a few weeks,

gathering flakes of dead matter
that I will slough absentmindedly
and without consent, from my tired body.
And when I am replete with good fat,
and the playlists, the writings, have been drained
entirely of sentiment, I will stick

the wad back in again, in its natural position,
and reinstate the whirring.
The hush-hush technology. The secret
monster of the neighbourhood. Boohoo.
I'd like to leave this room, and bin the notes.
My skin, which wants everything,
slips across the wet cobblestones at night,
looking for a friend to drape itself over,

while the bulk of myself, all of that pink matter,
skulks to the public library.
There, it will stew under the fluorescents
and chart endorphin spikes, engendered
by targeted spam, and then,
faced with articles on eschatology,
monitor the corresponding comedown.
Check the dailies. Check for vacancies.

We can't stomach any more application feedback.
The heating is shot, the carpets have been
warped by floodwater, and the Warden
is doing his crossword, with his head
in the clouds by the rail of donated coats.
The books are bloated like bodies,
and the fluorescents flicker. Rain,
more rain, is anticipated. Now we're really living.

Time to take this wilting thing off the hanger,
and slip into it, foot after awkward foot:
look, look how loud and competent I am
in my fully articulated human suit!
A real lover boy, with a manoeuvrable cache
of tragedy – *I've been losing so long!*
Best to get on my bike. Best to drag
the grapnels through my dreams, in search of content.

The line is being drawn; confrontation is necessary.
It is meticulously choreographed,
and a game of chance, all at once.
I wrote on Sickness, Scars, Cuts, Bruises, Care,
Invisible Labour, Emotional Meddling,
What It Means To Be A Body In The 21st Century,
Ammunition! Holy Grief! OCD!
Self-starvation! Solitude! Hire Me!

When I worm back out of the woodwork,
will you be waiting, and ask: buddy,
where have you been? Was it a pleasure?
Why are the backs of your ears so dirty?
Does my right honourable friend agree with me?
Why are you so quiet? Did you upset the order?
Show us your workings, try to remember
the words, the right kinds of words.

❡ There is no correct place to begin, or end.
Things don't square: KISS FM
on the car radio, during a funeral procession.
Driver, may we be dropped off here,
by the dog grooming parlour.
Or outside of Chicken Supreme. It's just,
I'm not in the mood for a ride in the country,
coasting through pools of light like water

along White Ennox Lane. Pull up
at the precinct, with the pitbulls
on chains, chewing stones. Their owners
chewing fags, their ends. Ah, the Esso.
Need baccy, actually, and love the smell of petrol.
Why don't we all alight at the Esso.
The vows of silence are becoming tiresome.
No one will call it what it is, or point out

the obvious omens: a run-over badger,
all its guts spilled and dragged across the road
by several sets of tyres. Smushed. Yuck.
For the funereal trim, the barber cut my ear,
almost lopped the whole lobe off.
Blood everywhere. I don't mean
to bother you, but this music is awful.
Driver. Turn it off. The radio. It doesn't square.

We're very far from where we began, aren't we.
It's been a very long day, hasn't it.
We must have scars somewhere, maybe
on our insides. Can't remember
what went wrong (*the trees have lives, the years
walk past on stilts, on fire*). A lot of drivel

has been peddled through the Firm,
and it's time to set the record straight, or try:

The family unit grew mildew.
Locked rooms, a spiritual machinery
operating in darkness, which required no fuel,
had no need for idols or pity, and had fantastic
and unsettling plans: keeping a close eye
on the mercury, doing everything, covertly,
to drive up the share price of emotional illiteracy,
the great British investment.

How easy it is to take advantage
of the ones who love you. How thoroughly
it can be done, and with such basic instruments.
Driver, what if we'd hit that little boy
who didn't think to look both ways
before he crossed the street? What if death
functioned like that, as a chain reaction?
Forget it. The weight won't let the right words out.

Circuits fried. Spilt milk. (*The pylons
are galloping crazily, the horse flies swarm the horse,
who hums.*) Light streams, streams down
the windscreen . . . the trees are wide awake
and phosphorescent. Their leaves are eyes,
very close and warm. The sky starts
letting itself, unexpectedly. Bells, birds,
are leaking from the sky. I have no escape plan.

Quick, I need some lines, the weight is killing.
There is a script on Wikipedia:

a crematorium is a machine in which
bodies are burned down to the bones,
eliminating all soft tissue. And the water
(there is a lot of water) gets evaporated.
These are the right kinds of words.
Nothing squares. Kill it please, the radio.

¶ The hand that moves the wheel turns the dial,
tipping cement into the conduit,
shutting the whole show down. A still lake.
A fine scum covering its surface. Under,
in the slime, deep nocturnal frequencies
leapfrog one another. On dry land
a wind-up toy marches around, filling in forms.
Red mist seeps through gaps in its panelling.

The monitors can't decide if spring has arrived.
It's in the air's texture – fits of sun
and rain – a withering thirst for warmth,
for the rickety scaffolding
of organs and limbs. It's an offensive climate,
which causes the water to freeze
and unfreeze, planting doubt that summer
ever happened, or will ever come again.

Clip, clop. Treetops smear green splotches
on the steamed-up taxi windows.
Upon whose shoulders is this car
being carried? *This wheel's on fire!*
Spring brings static on the radio,
legs of static stretching out, scuttling
into the ears. A Police Sergeant:
murder rates in the capital are skyrocketing.

And a Doctor: *this winter's been severe.*
Look at the excess mortality . . . Treetops are happy
bright headaches, however.
Scholars in gowns are slanting up the street,
the Socratic way, and getting on fine.

The Prime Minister [static] is pruning
the municipal trees, dumping
thousands of leaves across the pavements.

The taxi pulls into the hospital, as all taxis do,
eventually. At the desk, a real live human
begins to carry the conversation.
The cotton sleeve sticks, the fat perhaps
is seeping. Put a coin into the machine:
Good morning, images of rings inside trees
are absolutely terrifying. Good morning!
Churned, choked syllables spill from the mouth

like wet cement. *Is there anything else?*
Are you feeling quite yourself?
Sense of Self: collapsible/collapsed,
shatterable/shattered, clanking around
like loose change, in the cavity
behind the sternum. Interrupt me,
please, I ought to be interrupted.
The doctor will see you now; rapturous applause.

So [clipboard] *when did you first make plans?*
The cords are fragile. Clear the catarrh
from the throat, the gravel. I am myself,
just one octave lower, being rewound
at half-speed. There's debris on the needle.
Hands deep in pockets, scrounging around
for loose language, coming up short.
Is that a crow tapping at the window? God.

Well what can I tell you, the decent die, also
the just-good-enough, etc. What else.

We lived in an unfair town. Would get dumb
with weed, whatever, and gaze
at the dreamy valley mansions:
What parties they must have! [Classical poses.]
Our house was full of smashed crockery,
heather hung from the beams, perpetually

from the beams, dripping luck, not necessarily Good.
Sparrows nested under the roof tiling,
bees settled efficiently in the ceiling
above the bed, their geometric drone seeping
into dreams, making dreams quiver and blur,
dreams of blurry horses. Well, what can I say.
You end up sinking money into a house
and then it, and its inhabitants, are sunk.

Eventually all of us will answer a phone call
and thereafter be afraid of telephones.
Timber poles standing flush against treetops,
in dark red valleys, wrapped in vines,
their wires transferring ellipses which end
with extensions of sympathy . . . (Interrupt me?)
Hum. Life is very hard. There's no way
to articulate the terrible communal mesh.

Early this spring, a man approached me
by the fire escape, wrecked, to ask
where the nearest bridge was. I told him,
and the rain fell in itchy fingers. For weeks
I searched the local papers for suicides.
Clipboard. Hush. A slip of signed paper, thrust
into the palm. A glass of water.
A parcel to pick up, at the Nightingale Pharmacy.

¶ The wheel is doused. The years become,
abruptly, stilted: even, slightly,
suffocating. The years are on lockdown.
I don't let anybody touch me, or come near.
Frequently I wake with no clothes on,
and with the bedsheets stuffed
in my mouth, soaked in spittle.
I wake and think about the Firm, on benefits.

The many markings on the sluggish body
cease to be accounted for, rationally.
Each lash is coldly calculated
and barely felt. My body is forced
to come to terms with the idea
that the self will not, um, Let Up,
with its indulgent tinkerings and slicings,
its freely associative modifications.

A branch, tree limb, falls down the length
of the arm, as friendly beads eke out
from cleaving skin. The antique declension:
drippings, in stupefying patterns.
What would you call this, if you had
to put a name to it? A ladder with no rungs.
The mind is a golden animal, made of porcelain.
It sits in bits and pieces at the bottom.

A feather spins in a ceramic bowl of water.
The intuition has flatlined: anything
could be an omen, signifying anything.
In the supermarket, the discount trolley
causes lethargy to bloom and fill
the entire scope of the skull.

Fugitive drippings decamp from the cuff,
blotting the packets of powdered soup.

Outside, it's dark. A dog barks in the distance.
I'm pulled again by the tide,
toward the shores of Catatonia:
all the palms are petrified.
The mills were built, but never opened.
Old train schedules litter the dunes,
printed before the tracks were laid.
Water is the only thing that moves, surging

through cave systems far underground,
in figure eights, in ribbons, unheard on the surface,
with nowhere to go but back to its beginning.
A statue of the Squire, in armour,
stands on the hill holding a sceptre.
Light pours forth and retracts, like a spinal chord
whipped forward, furled back.
A dog barking. A storm. I'm sent, shivering, home.

I want someone to send me a message.
A message that would rattle the stacked glasses
on the sideboard, and turn loose
the tar from the brain. But there isn't anybody.
Anyway, my eyes don't have the strength to read.
The hour is bitter. Oh, Dearly Departed,
the weight is playing games with me again,
like a cat with all its little murders.

I've braced for it – *brace, brace* – like it says
in all the literature. But the bedroom
remains an enemy. Something's dribble

runs down the walls. Rabbits bolt from their holes,
and chase each other over the paper.
Damp, mildew, and dark water
have followed the Firm into every premises,
and won't quit even if the trail goes cold.

I can't stop staring at the spot on the ceiling.
It seems to be expanding. I think it might,
[creak] cave in, and the attic, all its stuffing,
suitcases, photos wrapped in plastic,
will fall catastrophically through.
The mass [bomb whistle] would be enough
to do me in. Thoroughly pancaked.
Do not alight. Is that what the Driver said?

Synapses warp and buckle, like rails
in ultra-heat, and every symbol
becomes indecipherable: circles
overlapping each other. Contorted faces
in the furniture. Ha, take off that mask,
it's not funny. Seriously. Alright already,
I get it, I haven't been taking care of my mentals.
Been a while since my last constitutional.

I agree with my right honourable friend.
But I'd rather not be taken to task
by a hallucination of the nightwatchman,
seesawing in the rocking chair:
I've a question about your credentials.
Have checked them against these character
statements, which say you do well
on the socials, and are affable in the workplace?

In fact, I haven't found anyone who can testify
to these ailments. Give me an eyeball witness.
Take me to the leak in the gasket.
The leak? The leak? We've all of us
been tanking our insides for decades,
if only our friends in the chambers
had the heart to take notice. Placards,
affidavits, testimonies compiled by several dozen

investigative journalists . . . None of it gets through.
The entire syndicate is against us,
and our own outfits are riddled
with infighting, unable to agree who, exactly,
is the enemy. We are our own enemy:
Mr and Mrs Average, on annual leave, got lost
in the bulrushes during off-season,
and stumbled upon the battered suitcase.

They peered inside, to find dossiers on each
and every citizen's physical and spiritual organs,
with extensive details on the precise,
idiosyncratic ways in which those organs
are flawed, can be manipulated, and made to suffer.
Thereafter, on account of the terror,
the couple agreed only to look out
for themselves, and even, in private, agreed

to sell the other in, if necessary. In my nightmare,
a family is trapped inside the cellar
of a farmhouse. Every member
has a key to the cellar door, but none will turn it,
for fear of first embarrassing the others,

with such decisiveness, and then
embarrassing themselves. A hole has been cut
out of the black velvet drapery of this dream.

It is the shape of a reared horse.
I crawl through it, and come alive much later
in the sun's silver heat, the bedsheets
soaked with sweat, with spittle,
and chewed clean through. There must be a mistake.
I regret it, the going inward, the reading
between the lines. The hand moves the dial,
looking for a different frequency.

¶ Various plastics float in circles, in the creek.
I wish them well. Sometimes, I am so in love
with the order. Dappled light, a drowned dove,
flies burning brown pinholes
in the air. The air thick as syrup. Treetops
are beautiful global skulls. The mower man
blasts away leaves with his leaf-blower,
and shoves me to my knees. I wish him well.

Formalities, after all, can rewire the hard drive:
simply force the heart to slow, and breathe,
quite casually, quite professionally,
as though you have been doing it all of your life.
Insert TAB A into SLOT B. Douse
the burning branch, separate the glass
from the plastics. File the invoices in good time
and line the toy soldiers, neatly, by rank.

Put several dents in your language faculty,
totally rid it of the vast number
of synonyms for 'fear' and 'wonder'
you have accrued. All in all, keep busy –
idle hands are the devil's workshop –
and stop. Thinking. I'm serious.
Watch as the weather picks up, and friends,
family, are pulled back into your orbit.

Solar-powered. Guiltless. Progressive. Wow.
Take photographs of each other.
Eventually, your life will be populated
with finer thoughts, which –
with some pruning! – will flourish
and even produce, good god, *feelings*.

I wish the Firm well, and write it a letter.
I drop depth-charges to the foot of the Firm.

My hair is freshly combed, and renewables sourced.
All my possessions are bundled
in the blotted handkerchief. The kerchief's tied
to the end of a stick. Stick's slung over the shoulder.
I'm a practical guy. *Goodbye*, I tell the mirror,
I'm leaving for the country.
I knock on my neighbours' doors,
and dare the men downstairs to call my bluff:

Goodbye, I'm leaving for the country! The bouquet
of sunflowers, wrapped in decades-old newspapers,
is shoved up against the windscreen.
The sun has siphoned itself out of them.
A statuette of a deity is suckered to the dash.
An excellent steer. Tree-topped and hat-racked trunks
line the avenue, striking up out of cement,
like the hands of earthen giants, with fingertips cut off

as punishment for stealing too much light
and CO_2. Their canopies are gone.
Their hollows hold secrets (*I have some pain*),
and secret wishes (*I have some pain*). Their eyes
will grow again. In another landscape.
Drive onward, along White Ennox Lane.
Call everybody's bluff: there are new kinds of words,
which grow with better leaves, in Canopy Country.

¶ Bite the tape and have it wrapped around
the wound, by sundown, buddy. Carvings;
white shirts. I have seen so many things, etc.
Hello, switchboard? *Get me the engineer.*
These toy soldiers are covered in dust.
There is a weight that will not budge.
Switchboard switchboard, the tap in the basin
won't stop dripping. *I won't stop dripping.*

Debt, shifts. Winter is half the year every year,
the rest is a blend of haze and treetops.
Rota rota rota. The rain [laughter]
might look nice pummelling the fire escape.
The light and its lashes, drunk on the pane,
might look nice, and evergreens hold my attention
for a little while, but. The omens are always bad.
Inasmuch as good ones mistrusted. Rota rota rota.

Operator: – *you are third in the queue.* Stories
are useful. What happened: the unit unravelled
and its constituent parts slept in different rooms.
The Firm was found to have cooked its books.
I stopped being able to find things funny,
ha-ha funny, anyway. Several deaths
and their associated costs. A collapsed house.
A heartbroken person leaning against the trunk

of an oak, chewing ice, and tearing up clumps
of bloody grass and dirt. There was no more
talking back, except to walls. *When I grow up,
I want to be, Second In Queue.* Quotes are useful,
for the record: *I thought about my life choices,
and concluded that this was not a wise choice,*

but did it anyway, persons being frequently unwise.
I left a void cheque at the Nightingale Pharmacy.

The pills went in the river with the till.
The charm of the other options wore off;
I went out shopping for knives. Hesitation,
then digging in – a separation, hot butter,
of myself from myself. No part of me, actually,
thought this was a good idea. The vanishings
in the basin. The carvings have left
a bad pattern, like sleepers on a track. Ha.

Operator: *Hello?* Now I am first in line,
at last, and the inky expanse of my life –
with all its sinews and flares,
its memories of bare lightbulbs on night porches,
the ceaseless budgets and phones off hooks,
and euphoric, intolerable eruptions of love –
charges directly toward me, blurry horses.
Hello. Hi. There are some things I'd like to talk about, please.

The Traveller hasteth in the Evening

A key-change, unexpected on a Sunday afternoon,
a glimpse into supra-reality:
the lutist silvering her hair in the steam
from a steam grate, by the bandstand.
The invisible pane of jasmine scent, then phlegm.
Stone steps wend steeply beyond the terrace . . .
Lactic acid jams in the tissue . . .
My frigid soul is bottling it, but is carted regardless
by the dogged body, up the Lofty Hill,
from which the limbless streetlights, lanterns, are seen
to glitch across the curtained city . . .
At the summit I sit and kick off my shoes.

Like anybody's, my tights are laddered, and my socks need
    darning.
Like anybody's, my soul is wanting. It's serious.
It gets worn down to a blunt edge, and the body with it.
I still believe in its capacity to balloon, and embrace
every entity: animal, vegetable, mineral or spirit.
When one soul encounters another, they make a Venn diagram.
The overlap is the epicentre of fluency.
Just now, in fact, I can see a stranger
peering through the coin-operated telescope, her cap in hand.
I can see her soul yawn, and stretch out
to bubble-wrap the fox cubs playing among ant hills
down on the lower slopes. I see their souls yawn back.

Love Story: Discourse Goblins

Am I – I am, I guess – a discourse-
Bullshitter, in bed at ten a.m.
On a weekday, listening to you read
K-Punk, with uneasy joy?
Cereal-box-toy-criticism,
That's all I've got to give, ineloquently,
In reply. Everyone's creative outputs
Are in arrears. Not ours, since
They don't exist, except as hypothetical
High-yield potential. We could
Make it if we really wanted, we just
Don't wanna. For breakfast, I will extract
A tin of peaches from the airing cupboard,
My 'in case of Extreme Event' peaches.

I don't have much else to offer. Except
This chip on my shoulder, about
The Classics kids, their lengthy
Athletic educations, and ability
To make and acquire tastes. Sorry . . .
The bulk-bought Nescafé tastes bitter.
I read an article once that said it contained
Chemicals found in Roundup weedkiller.
Oh well. Come out from the reading,
Fold the corner of your page: I'm here,
Spooning natural yoghurt in an open shirt,
And haven't touched palm oil
Or any refined sugars in, what, six weeks.
My stomach feels very flat and ethical.

People we know are climbing to high places.
We'd love to partner with you, if you're ready
To win? We had high hopes, and,
Who knows, could've been content
Up there. But all the blue light, screen dreams,
Office hours in chain eateries,
Failure to dock at the fortunate isles
Of Fast, Free WiFi scooped us out.
Hey, look, we may be past our best.
Decommissioned. Not fit for purpose.
But we're *on it* as regards oblivion.
Please, accept this breakfast bowl.
Accept this cheap and ironclad cynicism.
We're not famous. I am completely in love.

Hymenaios

for H. & J.

The train went straight through and out the other side
of our well-equipped routines, the loyalty cards
and mouthwashes, the miscellaneous cables.
Each of us stuffed a bag with one change of clothes.
Cigarettes, one book that would go unread,
and glossy magazines, with photographs of canyons and gods.
At the station we stopped to buy preparatory vitamins.
The day began to follow a pattern of subliminal embroidery,
the outlines of conversations left unfilled –
a way of covering as much ground as possible.
Rivets that fastened the railway bridge rattled like loose teeth.
Everything is so green. This was what half of us
were used to, but frightened the others half to death.
At the chapel we slipped through the function-room kitchen
to the toilets, and changed into dresses and suits.
We felt small in them, still young, like we'd raided
our mothers' and fathers' wardrobes. None knew
if our impersonations would pass. Either way, the clothes
would wind up grass-stained, or carelessly pissed on, burned.
Our arms were goose-pimpled in the changing.

The bride's nephew, just a toddler, acted as the ring bearer.
During the ceremony, he was frightened of the crowd
and ran backwards down the aisle, before starting over
with a new and dignified confidence. It was seen as a sign,
as it was seen as a sign on the Stag weekend,
months ago, when the only fish caught was hooked by the most
handsome, most dazzling and least punctual of us all.

There would be, we interpreted, great joy: indirect, unsaddled
with analysis, ulterior motives, or the need to repeat
some wrong done to every member, many years before.
Now we have it from the horse's mouth. Now we know
that the real love of two people can reach a particular tenor,
and transmute, so that it seems to discolour
the threads that bind the air in a room.
It gets carried, in currents, and alights on the heads
of patient bystanders, the heads of dandelions,
much as dust is lifted from a desert in spirals,
in chapters, and days later is dropped
on the streets of a distant city, with the usual rain.
Looked at from certain angles, it catches light and radiates.

There was a point in time when our sense of such things
was theoretical, or guessed-at. When we read Salinger,
we liked how Buddy finds the message that Boo Boo,
his sister, has written on the bathroom mirror
with a soap-inked finger: *raise high the roof-beam, carpenters*.
We didn't know what it meant; what mattered was the miracle
of the writing's still being visible.
How it had carried over, through flesh, fat,
silver and water vapour. During the speeches,
everybody is an unembarrassed mess, leaning against
the serve-yourself pasta buffet table, or standing
silhouetted at the marquee's edge, arms around shoulders
in an unbroken chain. There are no summaries,
or sleeves. The speeches grow and fill the tent.
There is time enough. This much we can give.
Plastic cups, of not-cheap but not-expensive Scotch,

are duly knocked, then spilled and cast aside.
The highest friend of the bride kneels to rethread a lace
through its eyelet. Then accepts a piggyback ride.
Together, they chase a ball kicked over the wet grass.

Tree Cutting

The red signs in the ancient woodland, near the ruins, say TREE CUTTING. As you proceed along the path, you can hear timber splitting, the dog-pant of handsaws grinding back and forth. The leaf-sodden mud is specked with wood dust. Soon, this becomes a thickened, beer-head scum, turning the earth the colour of snow and animal urine. And like snow, the dust seems to deaden all sound. Your footprints are the only tracks to pattern it. There are piles of branches, like tangled coat hangers, on either side of the path. There are neat stacks of freshly cut logs, with perfectly flat, perfectly white moon-faces.

You come to a clearing. Handsaws, mallets, and work gloves are scattered on the ground. Helmets, with safety goggles snapped onto the rims, lie here and there, as though they have been rolled off their respective heads without care or reason. The scent of woodsmoke hangs in the air. But there's no fire. Everything is very still. Then, up ahead, the evergreen tree-line bends backwards in a sudden wall of wind. Clouds flare across the domed sky, draining the little light that was left of the day. You have forgotten what you came here for. The way back is unclear.

The Giant Wheel

Last winter a ferris wheel was erected in the town square.
It was called The Giant Wheel.
An advertising banner stretched between two oak trees,
with a quote from Shakespeare:
The Wheel has come full circle. I am here.
A sign by the ticket booth said
Anyone can ride The Giant Wheel! But you have to be *this* tall.

It was very popular. There were queues in even the worst weather.
The freezing rain, the sleet and gales.
Sometimes, The Giant Wheel came close to tipping over.
But everybody continued to ride.
Schoolchildren, the elderly, bricklayers and estate agents.
At the top, they looked out over the roofs and felt at ease.
When the Wheel tilted, they tilted with it.

Love Story: Crown of Love

There is too much grass to mow.
It's better to lie down in from time to time,
And get lost, clutching, for e.g.,
Your ankle, finally fitting a finger
Into the rim of your ear,
Finding dried blood there
From a miscellaneous fly sting
You might have picked at, and at. Show me
Where, exactly, inside of you
I can hide. I am desperate to hide,
Co-ordinates please, Jesus:
This is the most I have ever wanted.
Or, to peaceably scythe every false growth,
And grow again, from the inside out.

The tree-brains are shedding their pollen.
I am shedding all pretences, refining
My attentions. In a moment
Of lucidity, watching a black ant
Move up your knee, I am convinced
We could bury the artefacts
Of our respective sicknesses, back there
In the vegetable patch, to be nourished
By common minerals, and evolve.
Is this bad taste, selfish, the sense that
There are no more problems left to solve?
Nix to the global crises, the endless
Ecological traumas. Just, don't care.
Let the engines float, then tumble through the air.

What I'm saying is, the chips are down:
I tasted the copper of your body
And instantly handed over all
Of my amulets, for you to evaluate
One by one, and tell me how
To lower my guard. God, I can't deal:
These sort of sickeningly lovely
Scarlet foxgloves in late June
Arrowing themselves at the house,
Stephin Merritt playing on your phone.
The real, actual, terrifying fact
That we've cleared the mesh
Of countless afternoons, and just like that,
Have fallen into it, on your parents' lawn.

AUTHOR'S NOTE

Each Love Story addresses a different 'you'. Some of these addressees are women; others are men.

ACKNOWLEDGEMENTS

I am grateful to the editors of the following publications, where early versions of some of these poems first appeared: *The Poetry Review*, *PAIN*, *Hotel*, and *Prototype*. I am grateful to Arts Council England for support in writing this book.

I am indebted to Emily Berry and Lucy Mercer, who read and advised on early versions of 'Treetops' and the Love Stories. Thank you to Declan Ryan for several years of guidance, direction and edits, and to Andrew Kidd for his advice and encouragement.

Thank you to my friends Oliver White and Katie da Cunha Lewin for their support. Thank you Joe Vaughan, Joe Summers, Charlie Case and Matt Davis for your imagination and creativity.

This book could never have been written without the love, generosity, strength and grace of my parents. Thank you to my dad (R.I.P.), and my mum.

Thank you, finally, to the dogs, Pixie and Scrumpy Jack (R.I.P.).